BRA... ACADEMY

CW00515160

Steph King
and
Richard Cooper

MATHS
CHALLENGES

MISSION FILE 2
For more able mathematicians in Year 3

Rising Stars UK Ltd, 7 Hatchers Mews, Bermondsey Street, London, SE1 3GS

www.risingstars-uk.com

Published in association with  National Association for Able Children in Education

Published 2014
Text, design and layout © Rising Stars UK Ltd. 2014

Authors: Steph King and Richard Cooper
Series Consultant: Cherri Moseley
Text design and typesetting: Steve Evans Design and Illustration
Cover design: Lon Chan, Words & Pictures Ltd, London
Publisher: Fiona Lazenby
Editorial: Lynette Woodward and Sparks Publishing Services, Ltd
Illustrations: Bill Greenhead (characters) and Steve Evans Design and Illustration

British Library Cataloguing in Publication Data.
A CIP record for this book is available from the British Library.

ISBN: 978-1-78339-230-8

Printed by Newnorth Print, Ltd. Bedford.

Pages 44–45, TASC: Thinking Actively in a Social Context © Belle Wallace 2004

Contents

Welcome to Brain Academy

Da Vinci

The master and founder of Brain Academy. Da Vinci has recently upgraded himself to 'tablet' form. He communicates via his touch screen but doesn't like being prodded and poked by Huxley. Da Vinci is dedicated to eradicating boring maths lessons and solving exciting mathematical problems around the world.

Huxley

Hux is DV's right-hand man. If he can't fix it, no-one can. Huxley carries a 'man-bag' which DV conveniently fits into. Always one for a joke or three, Huxley is the chap who keeps things moving in the right direction. Hopefully, forwards of course.

Rosa

Rosa Spudds is the Brain Academy gardening guru. There is nothing about gardening or 'growing your own' that Rosa doesn't know about. An expert in all fields. (And meadows, hedges, ponds, marshes and farms in general).

Hailey

Hailey Komet gained a PhD in Astrophysics at Oxford. She knows more about wormholes, black holes and any other holes one finds in the depths of the Universe than anyone else on our Planet. Hailey is convinced time travel is possible after the disappearance of the previous team ...

Evan

Evan Elpus is a young inventor from the Welsh Valleys. Da Vinci saw his potential after watching his on-line inventing tutorials, 'Elpus 'Elps You'. Followed everywhere by his Welsh Terrier Dylan, Evan is always up for a challenge. 'Tidy!' as he might say.

Omar

Omar Gosh is the world quiz champion after winning a global edition of 'Faster-mind'. He scored 100% and won on the last question. He knew how tall Mount Everest is ... in centimetres (884,800 cm). As a result, Omar's bank of useful (and useless) knowledge knows no heights.

Gammon

Gammon is the grandson of Ham, the Astro-chimp who flew into space back in 1961. Ham was trained by NASA to pilot a rocket. Gammon has inherited his grandfather's intelligence and has also developed the power of speech. However, this can sometimes be a little awkward due to his, let's say, 'choice of words'. He lives with Hailey Komet whom he 'adopted' earlier.

Mason

Mason Stones is a brilliant architect and master of materials, design and space. He can make any building, anywhere. His constructions are built to survive the elements so hurricanes, tsunamis, volcanoes and earthquakes hold no fear for their occupants. That's his theory anyway – he's still drawing up the plans.

Babs

Ms Barbara 'Babs' Babbage is a distant cousin to Charles Babbage, the inventor of the first computer. Ms Babbage has her own micro-chip like mind which is faster than the zippiest broadband in her home county of Devon. Babs has an accent thicker than clotted cream and a heart as warm as tea.

Echo

Once the hippest chick around, these days **Echonia Plant** (**Echo** to her BA friends!) works at Brain Academy part-time when she's not standing as a Green Party MEP. She knows all there is to know about how HQ runs, so she organises and manages communications. She still heads out into the field for the occasional mission when a nature-loving eco-warrior is needed though!

WPC Gallop and PC Trott

WPC Gallop and PC Trott are fearless police officers who lend a helping hand to the Brain Academy team when criminals are on the loose. Their investigative skills are unparalleled.
They do more than just plod about, you know!

If you ever met the previous Brain Academy team, don't worry they're all okay – I think. They got lost in the Space-time continuum after one of Victor Blastov's 'Time Machine experiments' went wrong. It's just a matter of time before they get back I suppose ...

Working with Brain Academy

This tells you where and when each mission takes place. Read the introduction to find out what the problem is and what help the Brain Academy agents need from you.

Start with the Training Mission (TM). This will get you ready for the Main Mission. You will need to use your maths and reasoning skills and explain your thinking.

You will need to find information to help you solve the problems in tables, charts, graphs, and so on. Remember to look carefully!

MISSION 2.10 Make Way for Segway!

TIME: At the start
PLACE: At the Segway Track

The team organise a 'Segway Rally' for kids through the forest. They have to avoid all the animals that are wandering around freely.

I'd love one of these to go shopping on.

People might think you're having a 'funny turn'!

TM

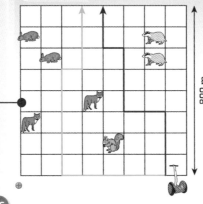

800 m

Two routes are planned through this part of the forest so the animals' habitats are not disturbed.

1) How many anti-clockwise quarter turns will be made on the red route?

2) How far is the blue route in metres? And in kilometres?

3) How much shorter is the red route in metres?

26

Now you've met the team, you are ready for your mission briefing!

MM

The winner of a new rally is the rider who gets the highest score in the fastest time. They must visit checkpoints along the way to build up their score.

1) What score does the rider get on the green route?

2) Find the difference between the scores on the pink and the green route.

3) Which route is best? Explain your thinking.

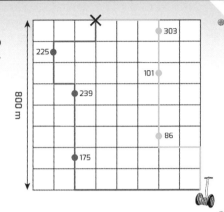

In the Main Mission (MM) you may need to use your answers from the Training Mission to help you. Read the questions carefully and think logically. What information do you have? What do you need to know? Can you use any patterns or rules to help you?

DV FILES

In the Segway Rally it takes the average rider $1\frac{1}{2}$ minutes to travel 100 m.

The riders are awarded a bonus of 25 points for every 1 minute faster they are than the rider who crosses the finish line next.

Using this information and what you already know about the pink and green routes, prove which route is the best one to take and find the winner of the rally.

I've ordered a segway for the Brain Academy Library!

Brilliant! It will get you from A to Z.

If you're brave enough, try a really tricky challenge from Da Vinci in the DV Files. You'll need to use different problem-solving strategies. It might help to talk to a partner or share ideas in a group.

Huxley's Helpline

Remember to use your answers from the Main Mission to help you.

27

If you get stuck, call Huxley's Helpline for a hint. There are more Mission Strategies to help you on pages 46 and 47, but have a go yourself first! Remember, Brain Academy agents never give up!

Ready for your first mission? Let's go!

2.1 That Sinking Feeling ...

TIME: *To hold your breath!*
PLACE: *Under the ocean*

The team have built a super submarine and are exploring the deepest place on Earth: the Mariana Trench. However, something's wrong with the sub's controls and Gammon the pilot is having difficulty ...

Gammon is piloting the sub. He's in a bit of trouble!

If anyone can steer that sub, Gammon can.

TM

Gammon guides the shaky sub into the depths of the western Pacific Ocean. The blue display shows how deep the submarine is now. The green display shows the maximum known depth of the Mariana Trench.

6 7 1 1 metres

1 0 9 1 1 metres

1) How many more metres must Gammon go down to reach a depth of 7000 m?

2) What is the difference in metres between the blue and green displays?

There is a loud bang and the sub is plunged into darkness.

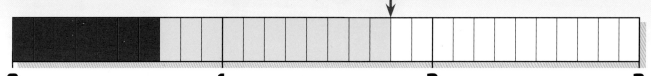

0   1   2   3

1) The power should be at $2\frac{1}{2}$ bars on this control panel. Where is the arrow pointing now?

2) Explain why Hailey has made a mistake.

3) How much more will the power have to drop to reach the red danger zone?

Oh, no! The power has already dropped $\frac{8}{10}$ of a bar!

Gammon gets into some very 'hairy' situations.

DV FILES

Panic breaks out at the surface, but Gammon keeps his cool. He remembers the emergency power packs in the engine room. But it is locked!

1) Use the clues below to find the five digits needed for the padlock code. Write them as the digits 1 to 9.

2) Now rearrange the digits to find the six possible codes that Gammon should try.

IX × I	VII – IV	XX ÷ V	XII ÷ III	XI – X

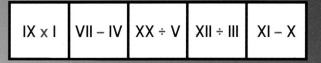

The last digit in the code is 10,000 times smaller than the first digit.

2.2 Don't Get Blown Away

TIME: *Hurricane Season*
PLACE: *In the eye of the storm*

The team have been given the task of flying into an oncoming hurricane to collect data. They need to find out where the storm is heading, when it will hit and how powerful it is.

It's feeling very windy everyone, hold tight!

Nothing to do with those Bean Burritos I made earlier folks.

TM

The team want to find out a bit more about hurricanes before they take on this mission!

1) Find out the direction that a hurricane will rotate around the 'eye' in Canada and Australia.

2) How many days are in the Atlantic hurricane season?

3) The Eastern Pacific hurricane season is longer than the Atlantic season. How many days longer?

Hurricanes

The Atlantic hurricane season starts on 1st June and ends on 30th November, but most hurricanes occur during the autumn.

The Eastern Pacific hurricane season starts on 15th May and ends on 30th November.

The centre of the storm or 'eye' is the calmest part. Hurricanes rotate in an anti-clockwise direction around an 'eye' in the Northern Hemisphere and a clockwise direction in the Southern Hemisphere.

The hurricane will arrive soon, so the team need to act quickly. The compass shows the direction that the hurricane is moving.

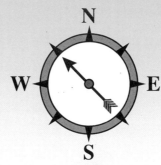

1) What direction does the compass show?

2) How can you describe the turn that would need to be made so that the compass points to the south east (SE)?

3) Evan thinks that the compass shows that the hurricane is heading towards Shady Shallows. Explain why he has made a mistake and why the team should race to Poppy Springs.

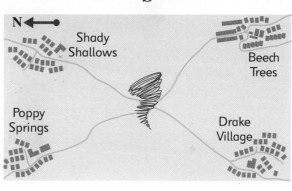

The map shows the towns that might be in danger.

DV FILES

TIME: 10:30 a.m.

A hurricane travels at speeds from 16 km to 32 km per hour.

1) Use this information to help the team calculate the shortest and longest possible distances the hurricane can travel in the given times.

2) Poppy Springs is 72 km away. What is the earliest and latest time that the hurricane might arrive at?

	In 3 hours	In 6 hours	In 7½ hours	In 10 hours	In 20 hours
16 km each hour					
32 km each hour					

Can you see a relationship between the shortest and longest distances each time?

2.3 Tomb Savers!

TIME: To get digging
PLACE: Under Brain Academy HQ

The team have discovered an ancient Celtic tomb whilst digging the foundations for an extended secret passage. They are investigating the treasure trove of artefacts.

Incredible; we've been sitting on this archaeological marvel for years!

We shall collect and record everything, Sir.

TM

Mason uses string to mark out three areas in the tomb where the ancient treasures were found.

1) Prove that Mason has some string left over from a 12 m long piece.

2) What is the length of the leftover piece?

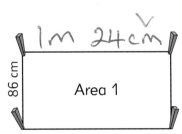

1m 24cm

86 cm

Area 1

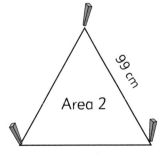

99 cm

Area 2

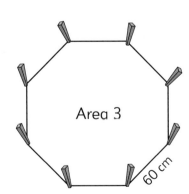

Area 3

60 cm

Items found in Area A

gold lamp   jewels   stone sculpture

Mason found 16 gold lamps in Area B. This is double the number found in Area A.

1) Find out the value of 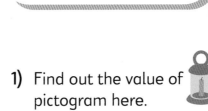 in the pictogram here.

2) The same scale is used for the other pieces. How many more jewels than precious stone sculptures were found in Area A?

3) There were 27 jewels found in Area C. How can this be shown on a pictogram where 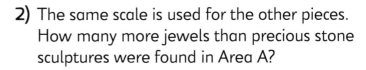 is equal to 6 jewels?

DV FILES

Mason weighs the treasures. Each gold lamp weighs 800 g and each sculpture weighs 400 g.

Find out the possible number of lamps and sculptures that are on this scale. Look for all solutions.

Digging for treasure rocks!

Remember to think about the number of grams in a kilogram.

TIME: Gammon's exhibition
PLACE: The Primate Modern Gallery

Gammon is having an exhibition of his artworks that he's painted. However, there is a thief on the loose ... the paintings are missing!

WhoOOO HAHAHas stolen my paintings?!

Don't worry Gammon, we have a way of tracking them to foil any monkey business.

TM

All the artworks are numbered with four digits and written in a book so pieces are easy to find and check. Here are five of Gammon's pieces.

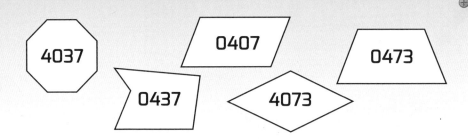

4037 0407 0473 0437 4073

1) Complete the information for Gammon's book, putting each piece in order starting from the smallest number.

Number	Number in words	Shape name

2) Another shape numbered 3708 has already been written in the book, but there is a mistake. Correct the mistake and draw the shape of the piece.

3708	Three thousand and seventy eight	Triangle with 3 acute angles

The pieces are being checked, but something is wrong! Several pieces are still missing from the exhibition! The police are called.

The square piece has the number on it that is halfway between 0735 and 0855.

The triangle piece has the number on it that is a third of the way from 0735 to 0855.

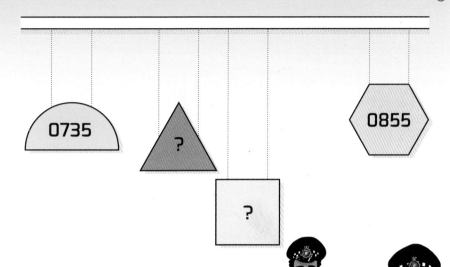

1) What are the numbers on each of the missing pieces? Show the calculations you used.

2) What is the difference between them?

The police are told that after the last full check that afternoon, the security guards patrolled the exhibition every quarter of an hour and all pieces were in the right place. Help the police to find the times that the security guards patrolled the exhibition and when Gammon's pieces of artwork must have been stolen.

3:43

Time at last full check | Time pieces reported as missing

I tried to doOoOoOoO a portrait of Grandpa Ham but he wouldn't sit still for long enough!

Huxley's Helpline

Think about how many minutes there are in a quarter of an hour.

TIME: *Lion o'clock in the morning*
PLACE: *The School Hall*

A litter of **six** unwanted lion cubs has been dropped off at the local primary school! However, they've escaped and will have to be rounded up by the teachers and the Brain Academy team: but how? The children are all moved to the safety of the Hall.

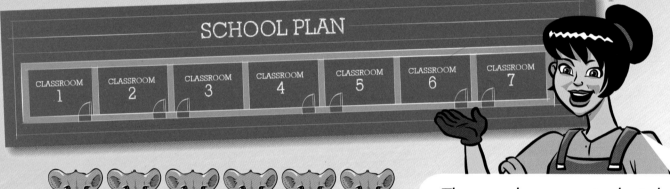

SCHOOL PLAN

| CLASSROOM 1 | CLASSROOM 2 | CLASSROOM 3 | CLASSROOM 4 | CLASSROOM 5 | CLASSROOM 6 | CLASSROOM 7 |

These cubs are cute, but deadly. Everyone be alert please. No 'lion' down and rolling over!

TM

But where are they in the school?

Use the clues to find the classrooms where the lion cubs could be hiding. How many different solutions can you find?

The lion cubs are only in **three** of the classrooms.

The cubs are **not** in classrooms that are **next** to each other.

The **only** classroom with **one** lion cub is the middle classroom.

There are fewer than four cubs in each classroom.

The team split up. Perhaps they can lure them out of the classroom with some tasty food.
They will use the same amount of food for each cub.

1) What different fractions of the food should they use for each of the three classrooms? Use one of your solutions from the Training Mission to help you.

2) How many kilograms of food should they use for the classroom with only one lion cub?

3) Use fractions to help explain why 12 kg of food will not be used in any classroom.

4) How many kilograms of food should be used in the other two classrooms?

ROAR!
Big Kitty Munchies
for lions, leopards and cheetahs
Serengeti flavour 18kg

DV FILES

Each of the cubs in this classroom step on at least three squares before reaching the food by the door.

The squares used by each cub make a number pattern.

Find the different patterns and the rules for three cubs. Use the ? to write in the missing numbers in the pattern.

35		29	19
70	90	49	
140	280	79	?
	?	1020	169
3240	2640	2040	Food

Door

One of the cubs was found behind the photocopier.

Ah, does that make him a copy-cat?!

Your knowledge of place value may help you here.

2.6 The 'Playground Games'

TIME: *Playtime*
PLACE: *The Playground 'Stadium'*

The plans have been drawn and the builders have started working on a stadium. The team start to design the games that will take place.

If this takes off, it could be bigger than the Olympics.

Indeed sir, it could be our very own Olympics for kids!

TM

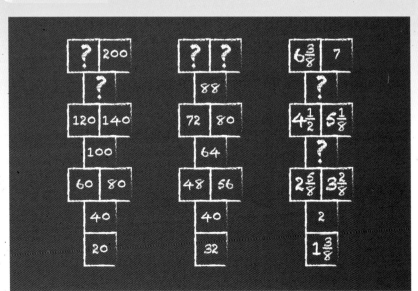

The team just cannot decide whose hopscotch design to use.

1) Find the rule for each of the number patterns on the hopscotches.

2) Find the value of the question marks (**?**) each time.

MM

The team decide to play a few games of conkers for fun. Huxley starts to draw a table to help them record the winner of each game.

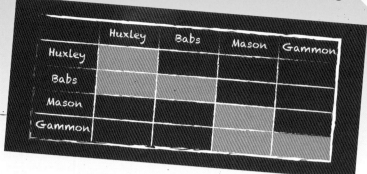

	Huxley	Babs	Mason	Gammon
Huxley				
Babs				
Mason				
Gammon				

1) Draw the table and complete the shading on it so that two team members will only play each other once. How many different games of conkers will be played?

2) Use this information to help you complete the table to show the possible results of all games.

	Huxley	Babs	Mason	Gammon
Huxley		Huxley	Huxley	Huxley

Huxley wins (all) his games.

Babs wins (one less) than Huxley.

Gammon (loses two) games.

DV FILES

The stadium is coming on well, but not all the games are finished.

In the game of 'It!' the chaser has to catch six children. They score the number of points for the zone a child is caught in.

Investigate to find out the following:

1) The highest possible score.

2) The lowest possible score.

3) The different ways the chaser can score a total of 390 points.

75 90
85
80
65 55

I'm excellent at 'Rock, Paper, Scissors.' but I do have trouble playing 'It'!

Try different combinations of scores. A table may help you to organise your results.

TIME: To get cleaning
PLACE: Outside the Shardome

The Brain Academy had been asked to clean the many windows of The 'Shardome': the latest tall building in London.

Ugh! I hate heights ...

I love climbing; I'll get this done in no time at all!

TM

Echo studies the two different types of windows to clean.

Window A

Window B

1) On which window can you see the greatest number of pairs of perpendicular lines?

2) How many more does this window have?

3) How many pairs of parallel lines are there on Window B?

4) How many acute angles can you see on Window B?

Gammon gets to work and starts to clean one of the Window Bs.

1) What fraction of Window B has been cleaned so far? Can you write this fraction in two different ways?

2) Find **three** different ways that the same fraction could have been cleaned on this window.

3) Gammon continues to clean the same fraction of the window each time. How many lots of this fraction will it take for $4\frac{3}{4}$ windows to be cleaned?

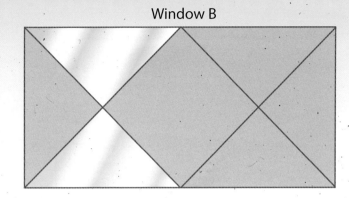

Window B

DV FILES

Gammon is at the highest part of the 'Shardome' building. To get clean water, he must lower himself to the bottom and then go back up.

Find out how many metres Gammon has travelled after each water change.

306 m

Shardome

After 1st change	After 2nd change	After 3rd change	After 4th change	After 5th change	After 10th change

I felt like King Kong when I was at the top! HaHaHa!

Remember that each change of water will require a return journey.

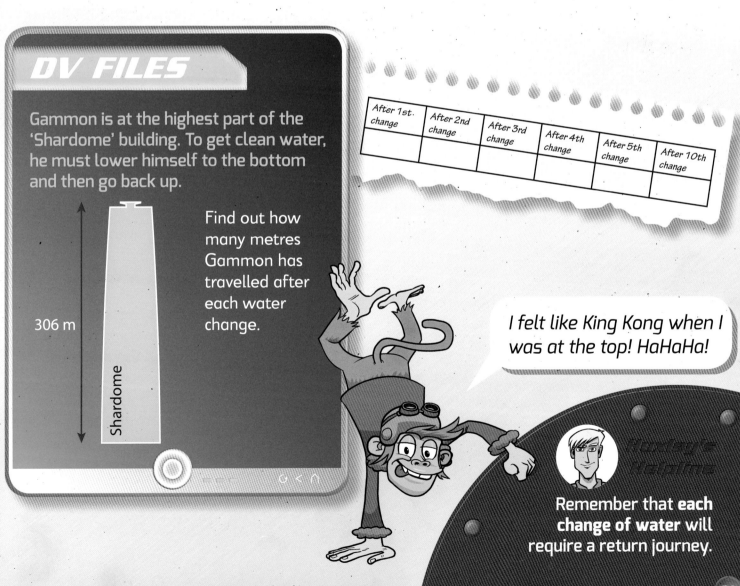

2.8 Balloon Race

TIME: _To take to the skies_
PLACE: _The White Cliffs of Dover_

The team have organised a Balloon Race. Different shaped hot-air balloons are lined up to cross the English Channel.

These balloons take some blowing up Huxley. Shouldn't be too difficult for you, young lad!

I think you'll find they're already full of hot air, Sir.

TM

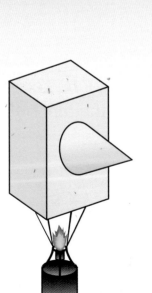

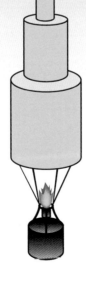

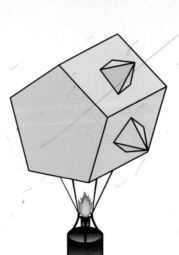

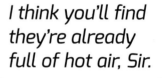

1) Name all the different shapes that make up the blue balloons.

2) What is the total number of rectangular faces on the balloons?

3) How many straight edges are on the balloons?

The route they are taking across the channel is a distance of 35km.

1) The balloons started the race at noon. The time now is shown on the clock here. How long has the race been going on?

2) **Balloon C** is travelling at a super-fast speed, but **Balloon A** is very slow. Use the picture to work out how far each balloon has travelled so far.

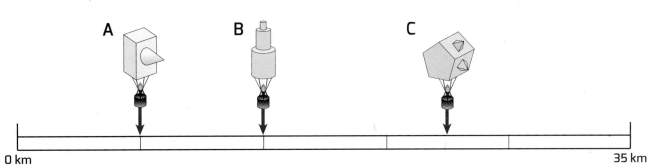

A   B   C

0 km   35 km

DV FILES

Balloon A wins a small prize of £180 for coming in last. Each member of the team will get an equal share of the money. There is an even number of people in the team. No one wins less than £15.

Prize money

Find out the different amounts of prize money each member could win.

I think I may enter the Balloon Race next year, Huxley.

Hmm. You'd better win and not 'let us down' Sir!

Huxley's Helpline

Drawing a table may help you to find all the solutions.

MISSION 2.9 Bathing for Birdies!

TIME: Bath time
PLACE: The Brain Academy Gardens

The team must design the new baths for small birds so they cannot be used by the cheeky squirrels who like to bathe in them on a summer's day ...

Our garden birds deserve the best, Evan.

My designs certainly aren't 'bird-brained', Rosa!

TM

Evan starts to draw some plans for the bird baths. Each one will have equal sections that start from a corner and meet in the middle at a small drinking bowl.

1) How many equal sections can Evan make in the hexagonal bath?

2) Find the difference between the number of equal sections in three octagonal baths and three pentagonal baths?

3) How many hexagonal baths will he need for 72 sections?

Evan has planned the baths so that each one can hold 3 litres of water in total.

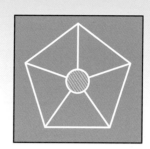

1) How many millilitres of water will be in each section of the pentagonal bath? Write the calculation you used to help you.

2) Now work out how much water will be in each section of the other two baths.

3) How many more millilitres are in each section of the pentagonal bath than in each section of the octagonal bath? Explain why you think this is.

DV FILES

The new baths should stop those cheeky squirrels! But when Rosa goes to check, she is greeted by an amazing scene ...

Find out:

1) What fraction of **each** bird bath is full of squirrels?

2) What fraction of a bird bath is left when Rosa tries to get all the squirrels into **just two** bird baths?

3) How can you describe the squirrel-free area using a mixed number?

Which birds always steal the soap from the bath?

The Robber Ducks of course!

Huxley's Helpline

A mixed number is made up of a whole number and a fraction, e.g. $2\frac{1}{4}$.

TIME: At the start
PLACE: At the Segway Track

The team organise a 'Segway Rally' for kids through the forest. They have to avoid all the animals that are wandering around freely.

I'd love one of these to go shopping on.

People might think you're having a 'funny turn'!

TM

800 m

Two routes are planned through this part of the forest so the animals' habitats are not disturbed.

1) How many anti-clockwise quarter turns will be made on the red route?

2) How far is the blue route in metres? And in kilometres?

3) How much shorter is the red route in metres?

26

The winner of a new rally is the rider who gets the highest score in the fastest time. They must visit checkpoints along the way to build up their score.

1) What score does the rider get on the green route?

2) Find the difference between the scores on the pink and the green route.

3) Which route is best? Explain your thinking.

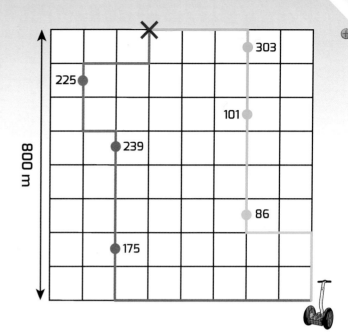

800 m

303
225
101
239
86
175

DV FILES

In the Segway Rally it takes the average rider 1½ minutes to travel 100 m.

The riders are awarded a bonus of 25 points for every 1 minute faster they are than the rider who crosses the finish line next.

Using this information and what you already know about the pink and green routes, prove which route is the best one to take and find the winner of the rally.

I've ordered a segway for the Brain Academy Library!

Brilliant! It will get you from A to Z.

Remember to use your answers from the Main Mission to help you.

2.11 Out of This World!

TIME: No time to lose!
PLACE: NASA HQ

NASA has asked Da Vinci for help to direct a space probe to land on a meteor that is going to hit the Moon. (They want to find out about what meteors are made of.) If it goes wrong, the meteor could hit Earth ...

Gammon's piloting skills might come in handy here. Are you up to it, young chimp?

YouHOOHOO bet sir!

TM

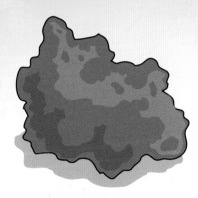

The team are fascinated with meteoroids, meteors and meteorites. They find out that a meteoroid is a piece of stony or metallic debris that travels in outer space. It becomes a meteor when it enters and heats up in the Earth's atmosphere. If it hits Earth, it is known as a meteorite – and the team really don't want that to happen!

1) The fastest meteoroid travels at 42 km per second. How far will it travel in 20 seconds?

2) A meteorite came through the roof of a house in Alabama in 1954. It weighed 19.84 kg. How many grams are in 0.84 kg?

3) The largest single meteorite was found in the USA in 1902. How many years ago was this?

1) The space probe is a distance of 2400 km from the Moon. How much closer is the meteor to the Moon than the space probe?

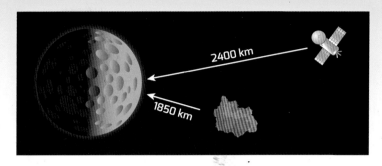

2) It takes the space probe the same length of time to travel 200 km as it does for the meteor to travel 150 km. Which one will reach the Moon first? Use the table to help you.

Probe	200 km	400 km
Meteor	150 km	

DV FILES

Gammon must now help NASA to remotely land the probe on the meteor.

Use the instructions **left**, **right**, **up** and **down** to direct the probe to land on the meteor: e.g. **left 2** will move it **two** squares to the **left**. But watch out for all the space meteoroids ...

Find two different solutions.

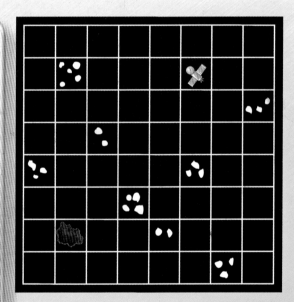

Gammon could land anything anywhere!

Especially at the *coughs* ... 'Hair-Port'.

Huxley's Helpline

Remember to say how many squares you want to move each time.

2.12 Running Robots!

TIME: *Testing time*
PLACE: *Evan's workshop*

Scientists have developed a number of robots that the Brain Academy team are testing to see how far they can throw and jump.

> *Well, I think I'm pressing all the right buttons ...*

> *How are you doing, Evan?*

> *Zap looks a little odd. I don't think it will be able to jump very far at all!*

TM

Evan starts by testing the latest robot inventions.

	Jump 1	Jump 2	Jump 3	Jump 4
ZID	$\frac{7}{10}$ of a metre	$\frac{4}{5}$ of a metre	$1\frac{1}{2}$ metres	
ZAP	50 cm	$\frac{8}{10}$ of a metre	$1\frac{50}{100}$ metres	

1) Find a way to prove which robot jumped the furthest each time.

2) In Jump 4, Zid jumped $\frac{25}{100}$ of a metre further than Zap.
   Zid jumped more than 2 m but less than 3 m. Find some possible results for Jump 4.

Evan now puts Zeb to the test. He wonders if this robot is any better. To his amazement, Zeb jumps further than Zid on every go!

1) Complete the table for Zeb. You will need to use your own answer from the Training Mission for Jump 4.

		Zeb's jump	
		m	cm
Jump 1	Double Zid's jump	m	cm
Jump 2	Four times further than Zid's jump	m	cm
Jump 3	Three times further than Zid's jump	m	cm
Jump 4	Five times further than Zid's jump	m	cm

DV FILES

In the last test, the robots had to throw a rock as far as they could.

1) Use the clues to find out the results.

2) Give all your answers in metres.

 −   = 150 cm

 +   = 900 cm

  = 7 metres

Huxley's Helpline

The length of the throw for each robot is the same in all of the clues, e.g. Zid in the first and second clue has the same value.

 2.13 Flowers in Space?!

TIME: Time flies in space!
PLACE: On the International Space Station (ISS)

Rosa is growing plants on the International Space Station. She's doing a series of experiments with a variety of newly discovered Amazonian species.

These plants have to work harder to grow because of the weightlessness in space.

More flower power needed then perhaps?

Five different plant species have been planted in coloured zones.

1) Write multiplication calculations to show the total number of plants in each of the coloured zones.

2) How many plants are there in total? Show the calculation you used to help you.

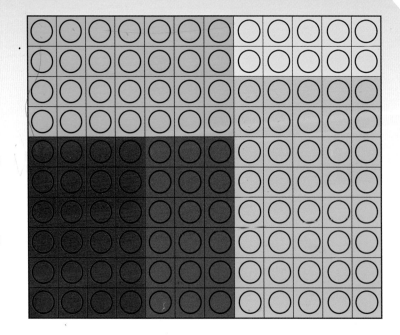

The bar charts compare the heights of one of the plants from each zone as it grows.

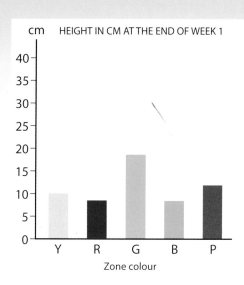

HEIGHT IN CM AT THE END OF WEEK 1

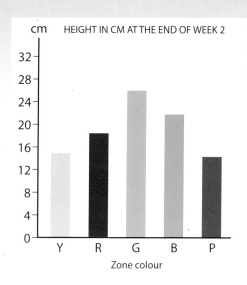

HEIGHT IN CM AT THE END OF WEEK 2

1) Write five different statements that compare the height of each plant in the two charts.

2) Rosa thinks that the plant in the **green** zone has grown the most.
Why does she think this? Explain why this is not true.

Rosa does different experiments on four plants at the end of Week 2. She wants to see what happens when the plants are exposed to very bright light and heat.

To her amazement they start to wobble and then jiggle and then move around, swapping places with each other! Investigate to find as many different positions for each of the plants as you can.

Two weeks on the ISS; what a treat!

An 'out of this world' experience, Rosa!

Here is one possible solution.

33

TIME: Deep mid-winter
PLACE: At the South Pole

Brain Academy have been asked to do some research on ice melting near the South Pole. Echo and Gammon have volunteered; as long as they can travel by dog sleds!

Brrrr! It's freezing out here. Have you caught a cold, Gammon?

Nope, but my voice is feeling a little husky hehehehe!

Each sled must carry 10 water containers: one for each dog. When the containers are empty, Echo and Gammon will melt snow to fill them up again.

1) The scale shows the amount of water needed to fill one of the small containers. How many millimetres of water is this?

2) How much water will be needed for all 10 small containers?

3) Round the amount to the **nearest whole litre**.

Echo and Gammon must remember to pack enough food for the dogs as well as for themselves. It is a long, long way to the South Pole …

1) How much heavier are **two** tins of *Doggy Delight* than **two** tins of *Top Dog*?

2) How many tins of *Top Dog* can be bought with a £20 note?

3) How many tins of *Doggy Delight* can be bought with a £20 note?

4) With the money left over from the £40, do they have enough to buy another tin of *Top Dog*? Prove your answer.

DV FILES

There are **10 dogs** on each sled. They each eat **1 kg** of food for their first meal. It is tiring work …

The dogs on Echo's sled only like *Top Dog*. The dogs on Gammon's sled only like *Doggy Delight*. Find out which sled of dogs is cheaper to feed for their first meal.

My dogs are really moving fast! 'Dog power' rocks.

OhOh! Mine are 'mush', 'mush' faster, Echo!

Huxley's Helpline

Remember to show how you have found your answer.

TIME: To read the timetable
PLACE: Brain Academy HQ

There is a new 'auto-pilot shuttle-rail system' that operates around the Brain Academy complex. At the moment it only has four stops. It's still been a headache to timetable it though ...

> My wooden computer can help out with this one.

> Indeed: it's got lots of 'bytes'. *Whispers* Probably woodworm bytes ...

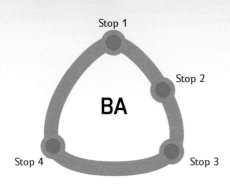

	Time
Stop 1	07:30
Stop 2	07:32
Stop 3	07:34
Stop 4	07:38
Stop 1	07:42

The Shuttle Rail has **four** stops. A full circuit takes **12 minutes** altogether.

1) At what time will the shuttle reach Stop 4 again?

2) Where will the shuttle be at **8** o'clock?

3) Huxley gets on at Stop 1 at **8:06** a.m. What time does he get off at Stop 4?

Babs and Huxley are working on the timetable for the rest of the day. The shuttle will not stop until after noon.

	Time
Stop 1	09:31
Stop 2	09:33
Stop 3	09:35
Stop 4	09:39
Stop 1	09:43

1) Huxley looks at the timetable and immediately knows that something is wrong. Why?

2) Correct the timetable for Babs and Huxley.
You may need to look back at the timetable in the Training Mission to help you.

3) Explain how many times the shuttle completes a circuit in 1 hour.

DV FILES

LOCATION: Stop 3

At 12:30pm, the shuttle stops running for 15 minutes. Babs is at **Stop 3**, but she needs to be back at **Stop 1** by **15:30**. Investigate to find the latest shuttle she can catch from **Stop 3**.

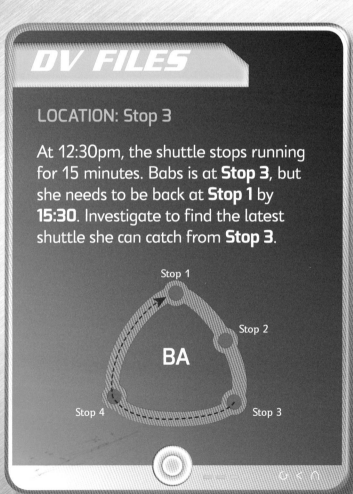

I've printed out a brand new timetable and put it on the web!

Use what you know about the 24-hour clock to help you.

TIME: Who knows?
PLACE: Da Vinci's office

Something has gone wrong with Da Vinci's internal clock system. He keeps switching on and off at the wrong times, with awkward and embarrassing consequences! Huxley tries to fix him.

Urgh! I feel dreadful – my insides are all crossed wires and stuck sockets.

You need a reboot and overhaul. Some servicing is required methinks.

TM

WEDNESDAY: Da Vinci was due to make a video call at 1 o'clock, but something is wrong. The clock shows the time now.

1) How many minutes late is Da Vinci?

2) Huxley checks Da Vinci's internal clock. It is **2½ hours** slow! What time does it show?

3) How long does Da Vinci think he has before he has to make the video call?

The timeline shows other things that Da Vinci must do that day.

14:30	16:05	19:29	22:35
Battery recharge	Meeting	Video call	Screen clean

1) How long is there between the battery recharge and the video call?

2) How long is there between the video call and the screen clean?

3) What will the time be on Da Vinci's internal clock when the meeting should start?

4) The meeting lasts for 68 minutes. What time will be on Da Vinci's internal clock now?

DV FILES

Disaster! Da Vinci's battery runs out in the middle of a video call with the President of the United States! They must work at record speed to reconnect the call using Da Vinci's back-up battery. They must reconnect in less than **3 minutes**!

The four bars on the battery must be fully charged before it will work. Only a fraction of the first bar is already charged. It takes 12 seconds for $\frac{1}{4}$ of a bar to charge. Will they make it in time?

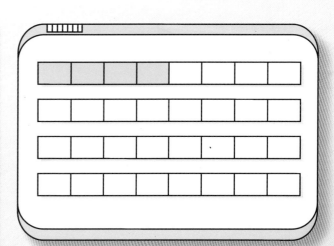

Think about how many seconds there are in a minute.

TIME: To go retro
PLACE: Ye Olde Toy Shoppe

Omar has inherited £10,000 from an old uncle! However, Omar can only have the money if it is spent on traditional toys for primary schools: nothing allowed with a screen. Space hoppers, board games, bikes, table tennis, skipping ropes and Old Arcade Pinball only. (Whatever that is?!)

Ten thousand pounds!

And what is wrong with 'screens' may I ask?

TM

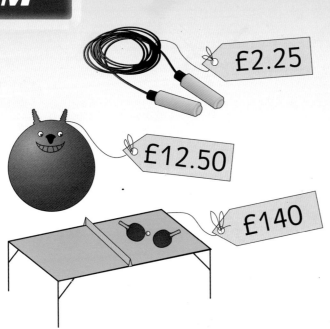

£2.25

£12.50

£140

Omar starts with £2000 and orders some of the games for the playground.

1) He orders **20** skipping ropes, **15** space hoppers and **10** table tennis tables. Calculate how much money he has spent so far.

2) How much of the first £2000 does he still have to spend?

The school children love the Old Arcade Pinball Games that Omar has bought them. They have already played several games. Use the clues to find out the points scored by each child with four balls.

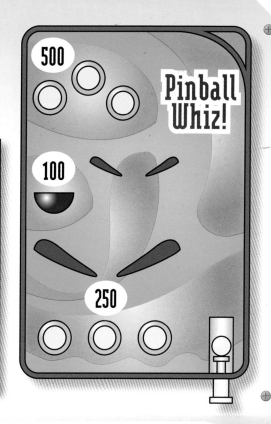

	Total points	Scored by getting
Sita	? points	500 + 250 + 250 + 0
Heather	$\frac{3}{4}$ of the points scored by Sita	
Alice	100 more than Heather	
James	$\frac{4}{10}$ of the points scored by Sita	
Leo	$\frac{2}{3}$ of the points scored by Heather	
Finley	Double the points scored by James	

| 5 children | 3 children | 4 children |

There are **3** skipping ropes, **3** space hoppers and **3** table tennis tables.

Arrange the games so that the same total number of children play in each **row**, **column** and **diagonal** in the grid that has been drawn on the playground.

These old toys are top fun. All I had to play with when I was a lad was a pocket calculator!

Look out for more than one solution!

2.18 Beetle Mania!

TIME: To start bugging folks
PLACE: In the jungle

The Brain Academy team are doing a survey of new species of beetle found in the Indonesian rainforest. Newly discovered beetles are found all the time. They need naming and classifying.

I've found two types of Beetle. I'm naming them Lennonlouse (L) and Maccamite (M).

I'm calling mine Ringopede (R). Still looking for a Georgiefly though ...

TM

1) How many bugs have been found in total?

2) How many more of Bug **M** were found than of Bug **L**?

3) In a pictogram where 1 picture = 6 bugs, how many of Bug **R** should be drawn?

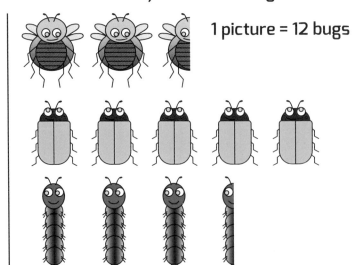

Number of newly discovered bugs found

1 picture = 12 bugs

MM

The team want to study the bugs' behaviour when music is played. Strangely, all of the bugs turn and move into a symmetrical pattern!

Rosa was not quick enough to take a photograph of the bugs in their new symmetrical pattern.

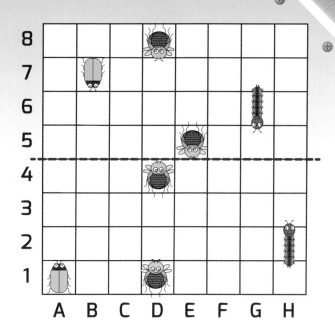

1) Try to move the least number of bugs possible to make a symmetrical pattern. Record your moves in your own way or as:
Move bug from D4 to ...

2) How many different ways can you describe the turn that the bug at D8 will need to make so it faces the same direction as the bug at D1?

DV FILES

Help each bug hop from a green hexagon to a red hexagon by landing on others along the way.

To land on a hexagon you must use **at least one** of the bug's numbers to write a multiplication calculation that has the same answer. For example, Bug L can hop onto 30 because this is 3 x 10 and 3 is one of its numbers.

3 or 7

4 or 9

6 or 8

Hexagons: 33, 90, 23, 140, 49, 42, 100, 27, 81, 108, 48, 34, 30, 72, 120, 57, 64

Did you hear about the two bed-bugs who met in the mattress?

They got married in the spring!

Huxley's Helpline

You can only move to a hexagon that is joined to the one you are on.

Problem-solving Strategies

Use the TASC Problem Solving Wheel to help you. TASC means Thinking Actively in a Social Context.

Learn from experience

Communicate

Reflect
What have I learned?

What have I learned?

Let's tell someone.

Communicate
Who can I tell?

Evaluate

How well did I do?

Evaluate
Did I succeed? Can I think of another way?

TA

Let's do it!

Implement
Now let me do it!

Implement

We can learn to be expert thinkers!

Gather/organise

Gather/organise
What do I know about this?

What do I know about this?

Identify

Identify
What is the task?

What is the task?

Generate

Generate
How many ideas can I think of?

How many ideas can I think of?

Decide

Decide
Which is the best idea?

Which is the best idea?

Mission Strategies

Mission 2.1

You may find it easier to write out each of the calculations in numbers first rather than in Roman Numerals. Try to be systematic so you do not miss any solutions, e.g. keeping one number in the same place and moving others around it.

Mission 2.2

You should have noticed that the Atlantic hurricane season and the Eastern Pacific hurricane season end on the same day. Think about how this can help you in the Training Mission.

Mission 2.3

Use what you know about 2-D shapes to help find any missing lengths on the shapes in the Training Mission. A table will help you find all the different possibilities in the Da Vinci Files and will make it easier to spot where you have missed a solution.

Mission 2.4

What is the time of the last full check on a digital clock? Approximately how many hours later were the pictures reported missing? The answers to these questions will help you with the Da Vinci Files!

Mission 2.5

In the Training Mission, you can use counters for the lion cubs and move them around a grid to help you. You may want to look at one clue at a time and try out some ideas.

Mission 2.6

You can use 6 counters to represent the children in the Da Vinci Files and then move them around to try out different possible scores. Try to be systematic and then record your results in a table.

Mission 2.7

Remember that using the square corner of a ruler or a book is a good way to check a right angle.

Mission 2.8

In the Training Mission, try to think about and imagine the sides of the solid shapes that you cannot see in the pictures. Have a go at answering all the questions before checking with solid shapes in the classroom.

Mission 2.9

Knowing how many millilitres there are in one litre will help you with the Main Mission. Also think about how your division facts can help you here.

Mission 2.10

Remember that clockwise describes a turn that moves in the same direction as the hands on a clock. So anti-clockwise is a turn in the opposite direction.

Mission 2.11

Look for number patterns to help you complete the table for the Main Mission.

Mission 2.12

When working on missing number problems like in this Da Vinci File, remember to read all clues or number sentences first so you can decide which one will be the most useful starting place.

Mission 2.13

When comparing the information shown on different charts or graphs, remember to check the scale on each one first. They will not always be the same!

Mission 2.14

In the Main Mission, you will need to think carefully about the number of tins that can be bought. Remember that they cannot buy part of a tin…

Mission 2.15

For the Da Vinci Files problem, remember that the shuttle stops at 12:30p.m. for 15 minutes. When will it start again?

Mission 2.16

It is useful to draw a number line to help you work with and calculate time. What size jumps can you make to help you?

Mission 2.17

In the Da Vinci Files, you may find it useful to sketch the grid and then move the numbers around it until you find a solution. This makes it easier to swap numbers without having to write them all out each time.

Mission 2.18

For the Da Vinci File problem, first think about the numbers in the grid that you know belong to the multiplication tables for 3, 4, 6, 7, 8 and 9.

National Association for Able Children in Education

What is NACE?

NACE, a registered charity founded in 1983, is the leading independent organisation for the education of the more able.

What does NACE do?

NACE specialises in working with teachers and schools to improve learning for the more able and to turn ability into achievement for all.

The NACE community provides teachers with:

A members' website including:
- Guidance and resources
- New to A,G&T
- Subject specific resources
- Specialist advice
- An award winning monthly E-bulletin packed with sources of inspiration and regular updates
- NACE Insight, a termly newsletter

How will the book help me?

The *Brain Academy* Maths Mission Files challenge and help you to become better at learning and a better mathematician by:
- thinking of and testing different solutions to problems
- making connections to what you already know
- working by yourself and with others
- expecting you to get better and to go on to the next book
- learning skills which you can use in other subjects and out of school.

We hope you enjoy the books!